No Thanks Mom

The Top Ten Objects Your Kids Do NOT Want

(and what to do with them)

by Elizabeth Stewart, Ph.D.

THE SAVVY APPRAISER

Author services by Kathleen Kaiser & Associates
www.KathleenKaiserAndAssociates.com

Publishing services by Pedernales Publishing, LLC
www.pedernalespublishing.com

Book interior and cover design: Jana Rade
jrade@impactstudioonline.com

Editing services by Erin Lenhert

Author photo by Santi Visalli

Cover and interior illustrations by Christine Brallier
www.christinebrallier.com

Library of Congress Control Number: 2017951659

ISBN 978-0-9981025-3-5 Paperback Edition
ISBN 978-0-9981025-4-2 Digital Edition

Printed in the United States of America

Contents

NO THANKS MOM

Author's
Introduction

The Philosophy of Ownership

Bringing it home

My aim in this book is to illustrate two important trends: first, that the value and significance of certain types of objects has changed in the past 30 years, and second, that those relegated objects symbolize a change in the meaning of value, especially with regards to what makes a comfortable home. I will show you, as lightheartedly as I can, that value is generationally related to the speed and mobility of life in the 21st century. I will share concrete examples of how parents have handled their Millennial children rejecting the things they wanted to pass on. I focus on Millennials because they are the group most indoctrinated in the new "lifestyle" value system: they were born into it, and were raised with its visual imagery.

The meaning of the once-precious "keepsake" lies both in its definition as an object and in the structure of the word. Words can provide clues to shifts in perception. The list that follows may have positive echoes and relevance for Boomers, but negative resonance and visualizations for Millennials. Consider this list with an ear to the double meanings of these words across two generations:

- ◆ Valuables
- ◆ Movables
- ◆ Goods
- ◆ Acquisitions

- Householdings
- Personalty
- Effects
- Furnishings
- Chattel
- Appointments
- Treasures
- Heirlooms
- Possessions
- Belongings

The professional case studies in this guide are examples of a shift in the meanings of the once-venerable and, in some cases, culturally ancient, words listed above. My examples come from my own clients who ask me what to do with their belongings once the kids have said no, and why, in fact, those kids did say no. The words that Boomers use when they cry on my shoulder are those above, which have long been used to describe certain traditionally hereditary material. For example, the word *belongings* comes from *belong*, which has its origins in the meaning "to be of long." It connotes possession of a thing as a natural member of a family, of a tribe, of a period in time. *Belongings* is an old word and is indicative of a certain cultural order. We still use the word today, but the concept of what a belonging is and what a belonging means is changing. A trend of the 21st century is visual compression: belonging to a tribe is seen not in terms of property to be owned or inherited, but in terms of pure life experience shared.

The culture we once experienced around material objects has changed significantly, reflecting the changes in late 20th- to early 21st-century values. This change in object relations is not new, but today is intensified. For example, consider the medieval word *household*. Modern houses no longer "hold," that is, keep or defend. And while a noble family might have moved furniture from keep to keep throughout the agricultural season, today's "movables" (the French for furniture is *le mobilier*) may not be portable enough to make it through your grown children's bi-coastal moves.

Here's another example of a change in a word over a few generations: notice how the old word *chattel*, meaning "possession," has fared. A historical definition reads that chattel is a thing held by a force or power: slaves were chattel. Another meaning of chattel has the inflection of noble status: an object held for oneself, provable of one's birthright. My grown son will tell you that he does not want to be a "slave" to the objects he is doomed to inherit; neither of the meanings of *chattel* has much significance to him and his generation.

As Boomers, our "effects" are sometimes viewed by our Millennial children as "affects." I think here of my young secretary suggesting that I would affect my 14-year-old son's future taste by decorating his bedroom with fancy French furniture. Our acquisitions seem to require Millennial time, energy, and self-possession, and may reveal a certain amount of moral judgment that young adults impose on their Boomer parents. In this way, the Millennial generation is not unlike the Reformer generation of the 1890s, which predicted a moral decline due to uncovered piano legs!

But this book is not about old history; it is about your history. Before you despair of feeling alone in hearing the words "No thanks, Mom," remember that the changing nature of life and its material possessions is not new. History has had its critics of materialism, none more brilliant, perhaps, than Dante, who wrote in 1472 in his *Inferno*, "All your possessions will meet their death, / Even as you will…" (translated, by Iris Origo).

One of the significant shifts in attitude toward value is how it is expressed. For those of us in the Boomer generation, we view our own history as narrative; as our book, as it were, not our movie. A Millennial views history compressed into an

image slideshow on a phone. Both viewpoints are valid. The distinction is in the concept of a person's individual and family history, which hits Boomers where it hurts: at home, which we see as an anchor. (By the way, your Millennials also see your home as an anchor!)

Here's the real meat of the matter: Do your objects really contain the essence of you? In the *Letters of John Keats*, by the great early 19th-century poet, there is a passage about an encounter with a material possession, the virtual material of personhood, seen as the vestige of a life, "which is like the relict garment of a Saint: the same and not the same: for the careful Monks patch and patch it: till there is not a thread of the original garment left, and still they show it for Saint Anthony's shirt." This passage suggests that the importance of an object lies not in the object itself, but in the embodiment of the object's cloak of meaning. That should give you some comfort. It's not about the thing; it is about what the image of the thing represents.

Thus, if you have picked up this book, you will soon be entering into discussions about the things that make up your home, but may not make it to your children's homes. Your distinct viewpoints come from two different lifestyles, times, and, indeed, philosophies about your objects, and neither opinion is less meaningful or valuable. The various keepsakes discussed in this book (for whose sake have they been kept—and why?) offer lessons about today's adjustment of values. The conversation requires you to listen to what lies beyond the words, with a greater understanding of an object's power in the symbolic representation of your past.

This guide was inspired by conversations (or lack thereof) about my keepsakes with my 30-year-old son, Lock, and his wife, as well as by similar conversations I've had with hundreds of Boomer clients and their Millennial heirs. I wish I had read this book before I sent many unwanted boxes to my son's house. Read my encounters with objects, Boomers, and Millennials with good humor, a few big cardboard boxes designated for donations, and a case of wine!

Elizabeth Stewart, Ph.D.

Santa Barbara, CA – 2017
Certified member, Appraisers Association of America

Author's china cabinet

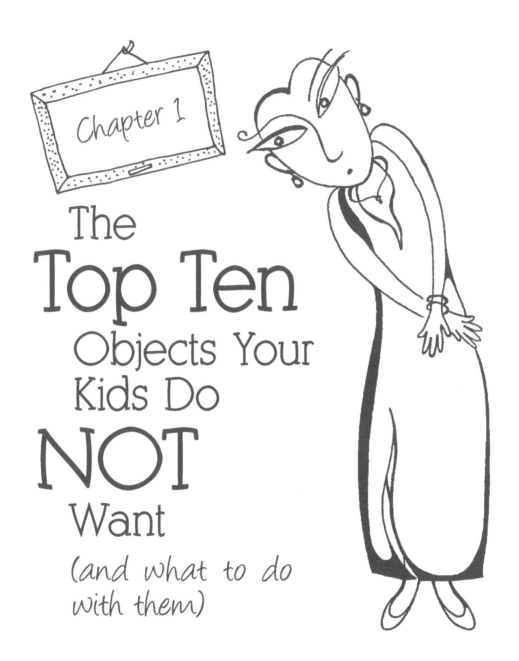

The Top Ten Objects Your Kids Do NOT Want

(and what to do with them)

Meredith,
daughter-in-law

Laughlin, son

Your house, and what it contains, is a minefield in the eyes of your grown children. They can see from your example that collections of stuff are a curse; such objects are superfluous to a life well lived. They want a clean, clear field in which to live their lives. Your grown children will not agree to be the recipients of your downsizing if it means their upsizing. As a professional appraiser, my clients who are parents have told me horror stories about trying to give fine objects to their kids and grandkids. In fact, I have a horror story to tell you myself (exaggerated accordingly for instructional and entertainment value!).

No sooner had my son announced his engagement than I ordered a pallet of moving boxes from U-Haul. My golden downsizing opportunity had arisen. I had been holding on to my treasures for the day when he could enjoy them in his own home in North Carolina.

The first set of 15 boxes I sent to my son and future daughter-in-law was my Minton formal china service, "Stanwood," professionally packed and Fed-Ex'd. Price: $679. Two weeks later, no word from my son and his fiancée. They must be overwhelmed with joy, I thought.

The second set of nine boxes was the Spode Christmas china and the matching crystal (with the little enameled Christmas trees), professionally packed and shipped. Price: $850. Still no word from my son.

Next, I shipped a set of pewter Old English Armorial Ware plates, 17 in all, with a family coat of arms (not our family's, but they looked impressive anyway). Pewter bends

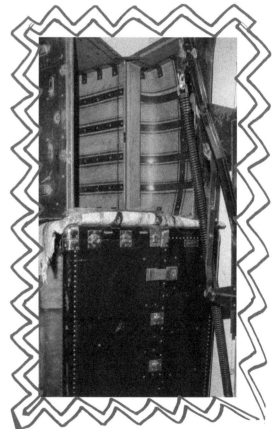

Your great-grandmother's steamer trunks

easily and can't be used or handled too much because of toxic lead content. Professionally packed in Styrofoam peanuts and shipped for $529. (My son is an environmentalist; the packaging with peanuts should be a clue as to how my downsizing tactics were being received).

Still no word from North Carolina. They are waiting for one more box, I thought. They're probably busy hanging up those armorial plates. I packed them a box of fine Persian prayer mats in various sizes; they were threadbare, proving their true antiquity, and the colors were muted with age and dust. Rare, impossible to walk on, and good examples of the lost art of the weaver. True treasures. I mailed those too.

Finally, word from North Carolina: my daughter-in-law, kindly but firmly, "Please STOP!!"

In my list of the Top Ten Objects Your Kids Do Not Want, I will help you find a remedy for dealing with each type of object. Here was my remedy for the above horror story. What I thought was my eagerly awaited downsizing opportunity became a minefield. I made the mistake of assuming that my son and daughter-in-law would want all the same objects I had wanted for a home in 1970s suburban America. For most young adults, this is not the case, so following these tips will help you maintain good relations with your kids.

Grab two tech-savvy friends; ask one to shoot a video, and the other to shoot still photos. The videographer will capture you touring your house, focusing on all the objects you might like your son and daughter-in-law to enjoy in their new house. In the video (that's their generation's medium), tell them the history of the object (known as provenance),

Your grandmother's electric fan

NO THANKS MOM

what you think it's worth, and how you used it or who used it. At the same time, ask the photographer to shoot a few shots of the object, and then move on to the next object you hope they'll want.

Write a letter, including a link to the video, and enclose the photo prints in the letter for a study-guide. Give your kids your requested timeline for their decision, maybe a few weeks. If they're undecided, offer to move objects to a storage area or locker for perhaps three months. Inform your kids that after three months you will sell or give away those objects unless they would like to help with storage fees (hah). Note: if any one gift is valued over $11,000, check with an accountant.

With this illustrative cautionary tale, I begin my countdown of the Top Ten Objects Your Kids Do Not Want, and some suggestions for getting rid of those unwanted things.

The Author and her Mom

John, photographer

#10 Books

The Steve Jobs aesthetic decrees a clean look for a home, without bookshelves or stacks of books on bedside tables, let alone piles of coffee table books in the living room. Unless your grown kids are professors, they don't want your books. There are a couple common mistakes my clients make in valuing books:

- The old 17th- to 19th-century books are not the most valuable. The 17th-century books are likely to be theological or grammar based, and are not rare. The 19th-century books are probably not in good condition, and since most 19th-century books came in a series or set, it's unlikely you'll have a full (valuable) set.
- First editions are valuable, and even more valuable if signed by the author. First editions rarely say "First Edition." But before you search for edition sequences, remember that the internet is not an expert on the valuation of books.

Remedy:

Books are a very special valuation object. It takes a real expert to know the great ones. If you think the book is relatively common, I suggest you plug the title, author, year of publication, and publisher into a search engine. Do NOT use eBay values. A favorite book site of mine is www.biblio.com. Once you have some background information, call a book antiquarian.

In the meantime, educate yourself on the importance of retaining dust covers and on the fine points of condition, which is often the ultimate determinate of value. You will save yourself time and money with a book expert.

#9 Paper ephemera

Family genealogy, historical papers, family snapshots, old greeting cards, playbills, and postcards are called paper ephemera. Some of my clients have engaged in sneak attacks to "save" these family archives; that is, mailing cardboard boxes to children without advance warning so that the parent avoids hearing, "Hang on to those photos a little longer, Mom." These are some common mistakes in valuing this class of objects:

- Old photos, even daguerreotypes, are not worth anything unless the sitter is a celebrity, the sitter is linked with an important historical event, or the subject is extremely macabre, like a death memorial image.
- Playbills are not treasured or valuable unless something incredible happened at the theater (think Lincoln at the Ford).
- Old greeting cards are not valuable unless hand-made by a famous artist, or sent by Jackie O.
- Postcards are valued mainly for the stamps.

Remedy:

Take all of your family snapshots and Super8 movies to a video conversion business and have them made into digital files. If you must give papers to your kids, scan them. Save the scans, not the boxes of paper. Donate the originals to the local historical society and take a tax write-off, if applicable.

The other option is to sell those old snapshots to greeting card publishers who use them on funny cards, or give family photos to image archive businesses like Getty. If the archive is a not-for-profit, take the donation write-off.

Finally, there's usually one family member who wants these objects, so give paper ephemera to "Aunt Kathleen" instead of your children. Your kids will be thrilled.

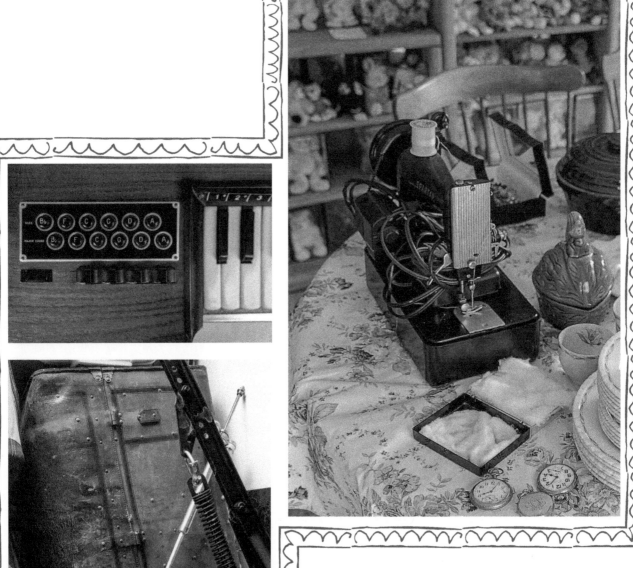

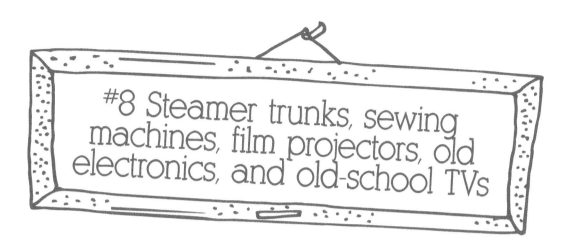

#8 Steamer trunks, sewing machines, film projectors, old electronics, and old-school TVs

Trust me, every family has at least three steamer trunks from the 19th century. They are so abundant out in object-land that they are not valuable, unless the maker is Louis Vuitton, Asprey, Goyard, or some other famous luggage house. They are "white elephants." Your grown kids will not be convinced that they will make great coffee tables or blanket storage, no matter how many magazine articles you show them touting the shabby chic aesthetic.

Likewise, every family has an old sewing machine. I have never found ONE that was rare enough to be valuable. And every family has a projector for home movies. Thrift stores are full of these items, so, unless your family member was a professional and the item is top-notch, yours can go there as well.

Even Deco console tube radios may not be welcomed into your children's homes. They take up space. Every family had a Zenith or Philco in 1940: they sell at auction for under $200. Only radio hobbyists relish the search for defunct vacuum tubes.

Remedy

Donate this category and don't look back.

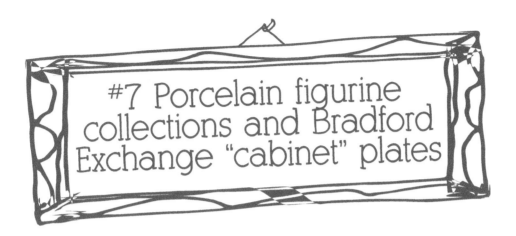

#7 Porcelain figurine collections and Bradford Exchange "cabinet" plates

These collections of frogs, chickens, bells, shoes, flowers, bees, trolls, ladies in big gowns, pirates, monks, figures on steins, dogs, horses, pigs, cars, babies, Hummel's, and Precious Moments are not desired by your grown children, grandchildren, or any other relation to you. Even though they are filled with memories of those who gave them to your mom or where your mom bought them, they have no market value. And they do not fit into the Zen-like tranquil aesthetic of a 20- or 30-something's home.

Remedy

Find a retirement home that does a gift exchange at Christmas and donate the figurines. If you want to hold on to a memory of your mom's collection, have a professional photographer set them up, light them well, and make a framed photo for your wall.

Collector's plates will not sell anywhere to anyone. Think "drunken Frisbee" or "Greek dinner party" if you dare send them to a grown child. Donate these to a retirement village as well or to anyone who will take them.

#6 Silver-plated objects

Your grown children will not polish silver-plate, this I can guarantee. If you give them covered casserole dishes, meat platters, candy dishes, serving bowls, tea services, gravy boats, butter dishes, and candelabra, you will be persona-non-grata. They might polish sterling silver flatware and objects, but they won't polish the silver-plated items that your mom entertained with and you saved. The exception may be silver-plated items from Cristofle, Tiffany, Cartier, Asprey, and other manufacturers of note. Check your local thrift store to see how much silver-plate they have and can't sell. This was a fad that will not be popular again, no matter how long you wait.

Remedy

None. Give it away to any place or person who will take it. There's no meltdown value for the miniscule amount of silver used to make these silver-plated objects. Across the board, silver-plate holds no value; it's cumbersome, little used, and smelly when tarnished. Get rid of it unless it carries a famous name. Note: a famous name is not "Rogers Brothers 1847." And no, the 1847 is not the year it was made. It is part of the company's full name.

NO THANKS MOM

#5 Heavy, dark, antique furniture

There is still a market for this sort of furniture, and that market, in the fashionable areas of the U.S., is most often the secondhand shop. You'll receive less than a quarter of purchase price if you sell on consignment in one of those shops. Unless your furniture is mid-century modern, there's a good chance you will have to pay someone to take it off your hands.

Remedy

Donate it and take a non-cash charitable contribution using fair market valuation (FMV). Often you can donate the piece for more than you can make selling it, and here's why: appraisers figure the hypothetical selling price for a donation based on fair market value across the nation. Even if you can only get $200 for your George III mahogany dresser, you could hypothetically sell it at auction on the East Coast for $1,000, and that might be the hypothetical FMV for a donation. Use reporting services such as www.P4A.com to find where this class of furniture sells. (Note: For a deduction, you must source what a thing sold for, not the offered price. For this reason, the offered price on eBay is a bad choice for research.)

#4 Persian rugs

The modern tranquility aimed for in the décor of the 20- to 30-somethings does not lend itself to a collection of multicolored (and sometimes threadbare) Persian rugs. This was a valuable market in the 1980s and it takes a trained eye to know if you have a rag or an antique treasure worth thousands.

Remedy

For Persian rugs, you need an expert, but the local rug dealers may not be honest with you. Have your rug evaluated by a certified appraiser: rugs are deceiving, because condition is not always a value indicator with fine antique rugs. The high-end market is still collecting in certain parts of the U.S. (think Martha's Vineyard), but unless the rug is rare, it is one of the hardest things to sell these days. If you think the value of the rug is below $2,000, it will be a hard sell; neighborhood sites like Craigslist have many used rugs.

Like antique furniture, it may be best to donate. If one market is strong and active, a donor can sometimes take the values from that market as fair market value. Prediction: since rugs are one-of-a-kind objets d'art that occurred in history, the market for Persian rugs will return. But how long can you hold on to those delicate moth-trapping rugs while the market slowly improves? (For nine years, my storage locker contained four extremely fine Persian rugs. Upon opening the locker, they were completely eaten away.)

NO THANKS MOM

#3
Linens

Go ahead, offer to send your daughter five boxes of hand-embroidered pillowcases, guest towels, napkins, and table linens. She might not even own an iron or ironing board, and she definitely doesn't set that kind of table. The market for these types of linens is poor because everyone over 50 has inherited something that a lady-ancestor "worked." When something is not rare, the value is low. And the young marrieds have no use for "his and her" pillowcases.

Remedy

Source those needlewomen who make handmade Christening clothes, wedding dresses, and quinceañera (Latin American equivalent of Sweet 16) gowns. Also, often you can donate those linens to costume shops of theaters and deduct the donation. A site like www.p4a.com has auction results to establish the fair market value of such objects, which means what the objects sold for, not the "offered" price.

#2 Sterling silver flatware and crystal wine services

Unless the scrap value for silver is high enough for a meltdown, matching sets of sterling flatware are hard to sell because they rarely go for "antique" value. The market is soft because formal entertaining is not a priority these days. Think about it: every married couple over 50 has at least one set of sterling flatware, so rarity as a value determinate is just not there. And of course, sterling must be hand washed and dried. It can't go in the dishwasher with the stainless flatware. Can you see your kids choosing to use the silver?

Same goes for crystal: Your cabinets probably contain a set of matching crystal that does not have a fancy name stamped on the base. In that set you have eight each of red wines, white wines, water goblets, cordials, and champagnes. They have etched patterns, or maybe colored glass accents. They are a "nice set." However, they will not be used by your grown children. They are too precious, and the wine they hold is too small a portion. Period.

Remedy

Sites like replacements.com offer matching services for folks who DO enjoy silver flatware and have recognized patterns. Because they sell per piece, and therefore buy per piece, sellers get a rather good price. Sell your whole silver service; it will be "pieced out."

Unless your crystal is indeed Lalique, Moser, Steuben, Baccarat, or another great name, you will not be able to sell your "nice set." Give "unknown maker" sets away, fast.

NO THANKS MOM

#1 Fine porcelain dinnerware

Your grown children may decline your offer of the Thanksgiving china service, the Christmas Spode dinner service, the Haviland passed down through your grandmother, and your own wedding service of Copeland. They may not want to store four sets of fancy porcelain dinnerware, and frankly don't see the glory in unpacking it once a year for a holiday or event. They don't want to hand-wash those gold-rimmed plates, and may even threaten to put them in the dishwasher or microwave.

This is the saddest story I have to tell my clients: your grown kids and grown grandkids DO NOT want and will NEVER want five or more fine china services. They don't even want one. They do not see the logic. They don't want porcelain tea sets or dessert, fish, or fruit services either. More than anything they do not want a set of matched (or worse, mismatched) teacups and saucers. Ask yourself, when was the last time you witnessed your grown son using a saucer?

Because your grown offspring fall between the ages of 25 and 50, they are now the buying market force. As a

Remedy

Like silverware, china is also something to consider for sale to a replacement matching service. Know your pattern to get a quote from such services. Because such replacement companies buy per piece, the aggregate of the selling price is always more than a bulk sale at a consignment store, which might be your only other option. The price paid to ship such services to another more promising market (i.e. England) is usually prohibitive. Donation of such services is difficult because the declared value of your donation must be based on real sales of a similar pattern. Try replacements.com.

group, this market force does not buy fine china, not even at bargain prices. Haviland Limoges, which sold in the 1980s and '90s for $1,000 to $2,000 for a five-piece place setting for 12, with vegetable dishes, platters, and covered bowls, will today sell for $150 to $200 for all of it! That's because 25- to 50-year-olds are not buying it at auction, at antique stores, at department stores, at jewelry stores. They are not buying "good china" anywhere.

Fables of Families Facing
the Top Ten Objects

Books

Nancy, a 28-year-old artist, tackles her mom's scholarly archive

Olive was a professor at a prestigious Midwestern university. In her 60th year of life, she was offered an endowed chair position on the East Coast. She began to gather up her library for a move from Chicago to New York. As a cultural anthropologist, Olive had weathered the waves of divergent authors and thinkers in her field, and she had gathered many of their voluminous tomes. Olive's library was in her home and was her home—four rooms of her Midwestern house were covered with tall bookcases, ranging all of the walls.

Olive's daughter was a studio artist. Nancy lived in Eugene, Oregon, and had a lively farmhouse studio with a large, well-loved kitchen-living room. And when Olive asked her, as Nancy knew she would, Nancy said she had no room for her mother's treasured volumes from the 1920s to 1940s, most of them signed first editions. Olive thought that those texts should never leave the family, but Nancy wanted her mother to donate them to her university. She wouldn't say so, however. Olive was a formidable woman.

Books are notoriously expensive to move, and Nancy knew from experience that they might not resell for much money on the secondhand market. She was a 28-year-old Millennial and was caught up in the gap between loving books as objects and loving books as digital readings. Nancy did love to occasionally hold a real book in her hands, loved the feel of a solid book, but she hated the weight and storage problems.

A reflection of her Millennial generation, Nancy thought that her mother's academic books offered a reader a chance to spend hours gaining esoteric knowledge of a topic in agonizing depth. Nancy was not particularly interested in learning about cultural anthropology in that depth, and if she wanted to look something up, the internet was a more convenient medium. For Nancy, learning was best accomplished through a series of images shown rather quickly. Or better yet, a video. This basic rift between the Boomer's approach to reading and the Millennial's approach to reading was difficult for both mother and daughter to understand. Olive wanted to keep those books

in the family, but she also wanted them to be read!

Nancy did a Google search for book appraisers in Chicago, as she thought that niche topics like existentialist cultural anthropology might sell for quite a significant amount to a select audience, and she needed professional help. If she could convince her mom to sell or donate the books, with real facts on paper, she wouldn't have to accept tons of books into her Oregon farmhouse.

The decision was made. Olive donated the books to the University of Chicago, and took the tax write-off. But Nancy had a trick up her sleeve. She flew in to visit her mom before the donation was shipped, and with the help of a new and wonderful app, she digitized those books going to the university. Her mom was grateful for Nancy's Millennial-style gift and took it in the spirit in which it was given.

Family Photos

34-year-old accountant David faces the family photos

Three boxes ranged against the wall of Joan's attic in the Chicagoland area. The boxes had three sets of magic marker labels: 1960-1970, 1970-1980, and 1980-1990.

Joan first took on a box of snapshots of little Joan and littler brother, Ernie, growing up in Illinois, dating back to the late 1950s and early 1960s. They were mainly black-and-white "snaps" with the month and year faintly printed in a pre-computer font along the crinkly white borders. Most of these were curled, as if they had been subjected to a "permanent wave" on a cardboard toilet paper roll.

By the mid 1960s, the stock used on those photos had grown thicker and more impressive, and though they had been in color, they were all collectively fading to a red-blue tonality. In most cases, the eyes of the kids and dogs still glowed devil-red from the flash bulb.

On the back of the snaps in the box labeled 1970-1980, Joan's Oma had written who was pictured and the event and date, and usually a joke about an older family member who might be half cut off, all penned in her spidery, Germanic-style handwriting.

On the photos of the holidays at the lake, even the dogs' names were included in the birthday party shots, and if the whole group was shot in the Chris-Craft motorboat, the man driving

the boat was named as "Cap'n." Perhaps Oma learned that expression from a Popeye cartoon or the front of a cereal box.

By the 1980s, the dominate themes were Joan and Ernie in high school and college, until two new little brothers began to appear. As subjects, Joan and Ernie were now a pair of blue-jean legs or a lap with a baby taking his bottle.

In the 1980-1990 box were Dad's Polaroids, with their padded edges that never quite relaxed into the thin white borders, and a bottom expanse of slick gray, impossible for a ballpoint pen. Oma had attempted to write the names and events on the back, but the ink had slid off even then. The Polaroids smelled weird and had faded drastically. On some, only ghosts remained.

The box from 1980 had a large stack of studio shots from Dresher's Fine Art Photography in Evanston, Illinois, where most of the upper-middle-class, North Shore German Jewish families had posed before a wedding. Those were the stiffest and largest items, mounted on heavy card stock with fake canvas texturing. There was a laminated article from the *Northbrook News* of July 1983: a picture of the entire wedding party in matching pastels.

Joan was selling the house, with its big attic and basement typical of the Midwest, and had bought a house in California close to her son David, who, like many Californians, did not have an attic or a basement. "So, David, do you want these three boxes of photos with the visions of your mother? Might be fun one day to see my fluctuations in weight."

The answer was definite: "No thanks, Mom. I have the vision of you today, and that's more than enough."

Steamer Trunks

Student nurse Elly, 26, ponders her great-grandmother's trunk

Elly's great-grandmother Sophia had declared, with feeling, in 1890: "So difficult to pack this steamer trunk without my maid!" Unwieldy, the trunk was three and a half feet high by four feet long, with a handsome brown leather exterior, across which spanned two beige leather straps. The interior was a colorful Aesthetic Movement geometric wallpaper, very *au courant*, a gift from a great-uncle for Sophia's birthday in 1889.

Sophia was packing for her first trip on a paddlewheel steamship. She would travel down the Mississippi, from St. Louis to New Orleans, to visit her older brother. The journey took three weeks, beginning the first of November. Sophia was glad for the trunk's commodious interior that held her long black wool winter coat, its over-cape, three large-brimmed matching winter hats in large round hatboxes, two pairs of black leather lace-up boots, and a new black silk umbrella. A separate section held four good wool afternoon dresses, one dinner dress, and three linen day dresses for the journey, and yet another section held undergarments. All was to be worn on the ship and throughout her month-long stay in New Orleans.

That long-ago trip had a happy ending—Sophia met her future husband in New Orleans and convinced him to move back to St. Louis. Thus, for three generations, that domed trunk

stood against basement and garage walls in St. Louis, then Chicago, then Milwaukee, and it was finally carted back to Chicago in the 21st century. No longer was the trunk used for the style of clothing for which it was designed, and no longer did porters and cable-hoists move trunks for passengers. The domed top kept other things from being stacked on its leather top, an advantage in its day (saving many a delicate hat inside), but an inconvenience for storage.

All Elly's mom could see to store inside were Elly's dad's Army blankets, which received frequent use. Elly loved to pull out those olive green blankets, smelling of mothballs, and swing them over the backyard clothesline, creating tearooms and forts. No more forts today, however; the trunk was filled with Christmas ornaments that had not seen a tree since 1970.

Now it was Elly's turn to place it against a wall of a house. Elly knew it weighed close to 50 pounds empty, and movers charge by weight these days. She knew that she would be moving house at least five times in as many years in her future career building. She was a student nurse at Cook County Hospital in the Chicago area, living on the eighth floor of a brownstone with two other nurses. On a student nurse salary, she not only had little space for the trunk, but nothing to store in it. Mom suggested Elly might receive Sophia's collections of handmade quilts and embroidered linens if she had nothing else for the dear old trunk, or perhaps somehow the three nurses could use it as a coffee table. But perhaps not with that dome.

"We'll discuss it," said Elly. But one of her roommates was an animal rights activist and tolerated no leather in the apartment. Taste, Elly's mom realized, had changed, and of course Elly never knew Sophia, nor was she interested in the history of early travel down the Mississippi. Truth be told, at 26, she had other interests, like dressing up for exciting Star Trek conventions.

"No thanks, Mom, I can't use that trunk, not even for my Trekkie costumes, just wouldn't work. 'Wouldn't be fitting, just wouldn't be fitting,'" she joked. A lifetime of travel ended for the steamer trunk with a quote from *Gone with the Wind*.

Porcelain Collector's Plates and Little Figurines

New York fashion photographer Randy, 38, downsizes wall plates and frogs

When Randy was forcibly downsizing his mom's California mobile home in 2017, he collected together a big cardboard box of 30 Bradford Exchange Limited Edition Special Mint Exclusive Premium Collector's Series Porcelain Picture Plates. His mom had long ago hung them on the kitchen walls of the double wide. Randy spent most of his morning rinsing the dust and congealed bacon grease remnants off the plates before wrapping them in newspaper. Then he poured a nip of brandy from the ancient bottle into the cold Starbucks coffee in the paper cup.

"What's next?" he thought. "What should I do with these?" He peeled from the great mass a few of the wire and spring hangers that his mom had used to mount the plates to the wall.

His mom had loved certain series of the Bradford Exchange Collector's Plates, notably the Princess Diana series and the Royal Family series, as well as the fairy tale plates, the famous ballerina plates, and the Norman Rockwell series. He put the huge cardboard box into his Range Rover outside.

One large bay window in the double wide had multiple shelves for ceramic and porcelain figurines. Randy saw with fondness his own little clay animals from fifth grade pottery class alongside her many turtles, roosters, and frogs. Randy counted 75 ceramic figures in all, and, upon further inspection, he did not find luminous names like Heuschenreuther, Herrend, Dresden, Meissen, or Minton. A few were Royal Crown Derby, which Randy googled and found they were worth less than the few Lladro figures.

Randy knew that each of those figures represented a birthday present or a special outing or a trip taken by his mom. It broke his heart, but he decided to bring home to New York City only 10 of those figures. Then he was seized by a brilliant idea. As he was a professional photographer for the fashion industry, he had a good camera and some lights in the Range Rover. He set up a makeshift white studio backdrop from an old sheet and shot a well-composed photo of the whole collection of figurines. Then he loaded the group into his car, drove to his mother's nursing home, and gave them to their thrift store. It broke his heart, but it was the right thing to do.

Silver-Plated Objects

Forest ranger Mari, 32, turns down her grandma's silver-plate

The wedding was small because the groom's mom couldn't muster the energy to fly from St. Louis to New York. The bride's relations made up the bulk of the wedding guests, but since she had attended college in Maine, not many of her friends could make it. The bride's mother wanted the appearance of a full church, so she had invited friends from her garden club, her bridge club, her church group, and her beauty parlor.

The church was full on that Saturday morning in June 1955—full of middle-aged, middle-class, East Coast club-ladies. Thus, the bride received 34 pieces of silver-plate hollowware, very popular in that era with that kind of lady. They included assorted serving pieces for the table, mostly with their own lids and covers.

The ladies attending the wedding entertained in a certain style, so they thought the bride would also enjoy serving bowls made especially for cranberry sauce, trays for shanks of meat with tunnels on the bottom for the juice, Pyrex pans with their own silver-plate holder for lasagna, covered casseroles with ceramic inserts, rectangular pans with little silver-plate galleys for meat loaf, strange half-moon silvered rounds for date nut loaf and cheese loaf, relish trays, and gravy boats. So much silver-plate!

Brands shown from the undersides: Rogers Brothers, Gorham, International Silver, and Paul Revere. Good, solid, American-made brands.

On one level, the ladies were right: the 34 pieces made a grand and sparkling display for the shower gift table once they were opened, but of course they were newly polished. Over the years, however, the bride became a mature wife with five kids, and she didn't use them much at all. One exception might have been the gravy boat, but that was good for so many occasions; her husband's uncle from New Jersey demanded gravy with everything.

The majority of the assorted silver-plated pieces, including the bun holder, the wine coolers, and the deviled egg platters, sat in a heap under the sink, and became dark and mottled with tarnish. Many of the larger pieces had been wrapped for years in dry cleaning bags and areas of silver plating had meshed and merged with the polycarbonate of the bags, creating a landscape of black ridges.

When the bride of 1955, whose name was Nell, planned a wedding shower for her daughter Julie in 1987, the silver-plate came out from under the sink. For some of the pieces, it was the first time they had emerged since 1955. Nell and her best pal, Rose, polished for days and resorted to Brillo only for the pieces that had merged with the plastic bags. The set made a nice buffet table for the picture of the wedding feast. Julie was not persuaded to take it to her new house in San Francisco, so the silver-plate again retired to its under-sink home.

When Julie's daughter Mari got engaged in 2010, the 34 pieces of silver-plate reemerged. They were polished again, this time single-handedly by Nell; Rose had died the previous year. Mari was called to come and witness the magnificent silver sheen for the first time. Mari brought her intended, Louise, and the couple explained that they liked the rustic woodsy life and could not tolerate the sheen of silver. Not only did Mari not want it at their wedding, she didn't want it at all.

Here's how she explained it to her grandmother: "Louise and I want to travel, Gramma. We don't want a house, we want a mobile home. Get rid of that stuff. We love you, but we don't love it."

Dark, Heavy Furniture

Emily's mom, 64, says goodbye to the family sideboard

Emily knew from her college history class that in a particular era in upper-middle-class America, families either had live-in service, like a maid and a cook, or, if they were a rung down the social ladder, maybe just a cook. Emily had learned that the form of furniture called a sideboard was a reflection of this trend; the sideboard was the main stage for the dinners prepared by the cook. The cook would sometimes use the sideboard to set out the family's meal in advance, so the sideboard had to be large, sturdy, and able to hold the trappings of a whole meal, including plates and silver.

Every family had such a piece of furniture—heavy, grand, usually mirrored at the backsplash to set off the fine porcelain serving dishes and the silver or silver-plated candelabra. The sideboard, or buffet, was usually oak, walnut, or mahogany, and it had a few drawers below the serving area, padded in green baize cloth for the silver service. The finest of this form had a marble top for the hot dishes. If a family could not afford marble, the counter space on a sideboard was large and deep enough for butler's trays. The two cabinet doors beneath held serving dishes, and the finest sideboards also had wine drawers for bottle storage.

These sideboards were to the dining room what the hearth was to the parlor: the center of attention, especially at meal times,

when they were way stations for the cook and the serving staff, a midpoint between the kitchen and the dining room. The sideboard was such an indispensable piece of furniture that at one time in the late 19th century, architects actually built them into the floor plan. Big, heavy, oppressive, and dark, sideboards were meant to groan with the plentitude of courses popular in the 19th and early 20th centuries. The pieces echoed the style of dining: formal, appropriately dressed, always on time, always lengthy, always seated, communal for the entire family, and multi-coursed.

Emily knew that Americans do not eat like that today! We do not need storage for fine silver and cut glass and porcelain serving pieces. Thus, when Emily and John moved out of her mother's maid's quarters in Boston to a little professor's bungalow in Berkeley (taking Mom, who had serious health issues), Emily knew she would be faced with Mom's reticence to leave the family sideboard behind. That sideboard had seen Christmases and christenings, wakes and weddings. Emily and John simply didn't have room.

John remembered fondly that his mother-in-law, in healthier days, had taken on lodgers in the big house. The sideboard became the focal point of the breakfast hour shared among guests. But now his teaching career was launched, he was making his own salary, and he wanted to furnish his own little house. The sideboard would not be welcome.

As she was interviewing realtors in Boston, Emily broke the news: "Mom, we have so many memories of your wonderful Christmas cakes on tall glass pedestals on that sideboard. We have pictures of your condolence cards ranged along the top shelf over the mirror when dad passed. We have evidence from the morning coffeepots and the heat rings from the hot plates. But, no thanks, Mom; we've got to leave it with the house." Mom looked at the sideboard's drawer pulls, polished by years of use. She would miss the old friend, a memory of formal meals long passed.

Persian Rugs

Hipster newlyweds decline fifty Persian rugs

Mary and Lawrence's restored farmhouse outside of Raleigh was a picture-perfect example of North Carolina style, a rare combination of 1920s Queen Anne grace and 2017 rustic elegance, rendered in the minimalist style. Nothing shone garishly and nothing glittered with tawdry silver or gold accents. If Mary brought home wildflowers, she set them on the simple, unadorned mantelpiece in an old blue-glass barber's bottle, one of their few antique pieces. The decor was peaceful and tasteful—grays, blues, beiges, creams, no saturated colors.

Lawrence had spent every weekend with his college buddies, sanding down the cedar floors. A light coat of oil revealed their simple reddish distress marks. Tiny, low-intensity, exposed light bulbs ranged along the joist of the walls, lighting sepia photos of ancient Buddhist temples. These pictures were taken from 1870 to 1900 by Mary's great-uncle, who had served during the Raj years in India. He had often taken his leave in the territory known as Persia, and he had collected flat-weave Persian rugs and other colorful tapestries, such as camel saddles. These 50 or so rugs were left to Mary's mom, and Mary knew she would have to decide their fate.

After Mary's dad died, her mom decided to move and began to downsize the huge Victorian in Seattle fitted out with 18th-century English furniture. The phone call from Seattle finally came: "Mary, you and Lawrence need to take these Persian rugs off my hands. Eventually you might live in a house that would fit them. Yes or no?"

Lawrence, who was from the South, asked, "How much are they worth, Big Mom?"

Mom said: "How should I know? They've been on the floor for 40 or 50 years."

Holding the phone in a cupped hand, Mary said to Lawrence "Do we really want all those colors all over our refinished floors? And think of the cats!"

Mary remembered the time she had slipped on one of them, when her mom had neglected to tape it securely to the floor with that messy double-sided tape. An exasperated silence ensued.

"No thanks, Mom, but I am sure Lawrence would help you sell them when he comes to Seattle on business next month."

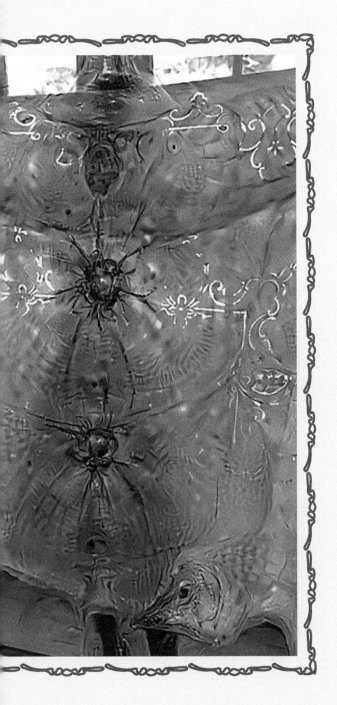

Linens

Millenials Maggie and Lisa despair of Great-Aunt Rebecca's linens

Laura, a mother of two 20-somethings, found a letter in an old suitcase in her late mother's attic. The case was full of pockmarked antique linens, which had once been snow white with bluing, the pride of her great-aunt's table and lovely down beds. Pulling out the linens, the variety of forms astounded Laura: dinner-sized embossed linen napkins embroidered with the family "S"; hand-hemmed, supper-sized, lighter-weight napkins embroidered with miniature horses in a nod to the stables beyond the big house; and cocktail napkins folded directly in half with little crowing cocks sewn into the corners. Each suite of these napkins was accompanied by two matching tablecloths with similar motifs. Laura's favorite was the "Cocktail Time" tablecloth with a colorful fat hen; from her beak rose a cartoon bubble proclaiming "Have a peck!" in red deco-style embroidery.

The bed linens, on the other hand, were so lacy and feminine that she could not picture her great-uncle inside them. The counterpanes boasted of the skill of the long-past needlewomen who created a trousseau for her great-aunt. There was Battenberg lace to the edges and interior cartouches of crochet or pulled work that accented the collection. Two sets of six pillowcases: one proclaimed "HIS" and the other "HERS." One set of pillowcases was much more formal, with an interlocking monogram of her great-uncle, "VSE." Both sets had matching flat sheets in what today is marketed as double size. Laura noticed there were no fitted bottom sheets, as that was a much later development in the bed linen world.

The letter?

"Dear Niece,

You were just a baby when I went into the nursing home; I want you to have these, and gave this case to your mom to hide in her attic for you to find one day. I will be long gone when you open this suitcase! Before I married your great-uncle Vernon, my cousins Theresa and Cecelia, supervised by their mother, Aunt Kathleen, learned proper needlework upon these, my wedding linens. Every Sunday, as I remember, after church we would sit and sew, for at least a year before my wedding in 1929. And all of us cousins returned the favor: I sat and sewed for Theresa's trousseau, even though I was expecting your Uncle George. For Ceci, we sewed underclothes, as by that time Ceci had inherited her mother's trousseau. Please enjoy these and pass them to your daughter, if you are lucky enough to have one. Vernon and I did not.
Love, your Great-Aunt Rebecca"

Laura's first thought was "What am I going to do with all these?" She called her daughters, Maggie, a drama instructor in Michigan, and Lisa, a nursing assistant in Richmond. "Let's divide these amongst us! I can send some out! Let me know if you want table linens, bed linens, bathroom linens, or handkerchiefs. There's about 20 in each category."

Dead silence on the call. Maggie spoke first: "No thanks, Mom." Then a few seconds later, Lisa: "Wow, Mom, no thanks." And nothing more.

Crystal Sets and Formal Flatware

Kelly, a working urban mom, takes the crystal but dumps the silver

Kelly knew that in her grandmother's day, a common wedding present was a beverage service for 12 in patterned pressed glass or clear glass etched with flowers and Greek key designs. Kelly was turning 35, and all of her friends were asking each other if they knew anything about the glass sets they had been receiving from their downsizing moms. Long stored on shelves at the back of the fancy china cabinet, getting sootier each year, Kelly's grandmother's glasses finally needed to be packed up. The sets had originally included 12 each of white wines, red wines, waters, cordials, and boat-shaped champagnes, but they were delicate glass, so there were now five or six of most types. Kelly's mom had sent her a picture, asking if Kelly wanted what remained of the set. Why not, thought Kelly, there aren't that many.

Looking at it from a historical lens, the history of American attitudes toward booze is hidden in the portion size of these glasses. In the first quarter of the 20th century, beverage sets primarily included wine glasses, especially in homes of European ancestry. Wine glasses were simple, with sides that flared outward or were straight, unlike today's glasses that curve inward to contain the wine's bouquet. Although the alcohol content of wine has not changed, the portion size in those antique sets is three to four ounces. In 1930, the heyday

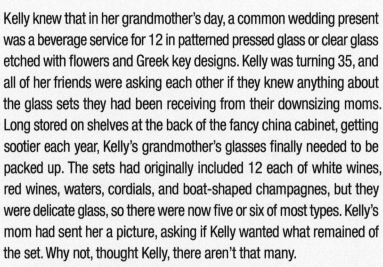

of cocktails, these sets did not necessarily contain the forms we associate with wines; they were more likely to include new favorite cocktail receptacles such as the highball glass, the sours glass, and the martini glass. By the 1940s, cocktail glasses joined wine and water glasses in the matching set, and the full beverage service in one pattern was born as the essential wedding present.

Kelly received the truncated set. The champagnes, Kelly thought, are the most curious, as these long low bowls are not easy to drink from and the champagne seems to slosh everywhere in a toast. Those boat shapes meant that the champagne had a maximum surface area exposed to the air, and more bubbles were shown on the surface. Kelly used these for her kid's sherbet or her bridge club's shrimp cocktails. She didn't like the bubbles in her nose.

Kelly and her girlfriends who have inherited such sets hardly use them and they scoff at their forebears who drank wine in three- to four-ounce portions. Kelly has tried to sell her grandmother's set on eBay and has found that there's no demand, especially since the set is incomplete and is not Tiffany, Baccarat, or Moser. Millennials value functionality, utility, and ease of maintenance, so these sets have limited value. They are a delicate example of drinking alcohol in moderation on special occasions, not exactly what Kelly thinks of as appropriate for her wine connoisseur husband.

A close cousin to the formal beverage service is Kelly's grandparents' sets of formal sterling flatware. Kelly's mom inherited sterling from grandparents on both sides of her family. She would like to give Kelly the Alvin set and the Gorham set,

which both hail from mid-century America. Kelly won't tell her mom, but she would like to have them to sell, because she has heard that the meltdown value of the silver is worth more than the sets sold as a silver service. The jewelry shop where Kelly asked about meltdown told her that pre-1930 sterling sets were made with more sterling, the patterns were chased in more dramatic relief, and they feel more balanced and weighty in the hand. Those sets have value in the antique marketplace, but not the mid-century sets with their vapid flowers.

Kelly has decided; she doesn't want the sterling. She is afraid to put them with stainless in the dishwasher and she has already envisioned herself mistakenly putting one down the garbage disposal. Her mom had suggested that Kelly get rid of her stainless and use the good sterling flatware every day, but Kelly's daughter says that when she eats at Grandma's with a sterling spoon, she hates the taste. Also, there's the time-waster of polishing silver.

The tastemakers that Kelly follows on Instagram have not raved about silver, nor suggested multiple sets of flatware for those new "challenge recipe" group parties. Kelly explained, "I want to humble-brag about my functional and utilitarian, yet stylish and eclectic ranch-style kitchen, and sterling silver flatware will not make the cut, Mom."

Mom's comment? "What the hell is humble-brag?"

Formal China

Loft-dwellers Stephie and Peter say NO to formal dinnerware

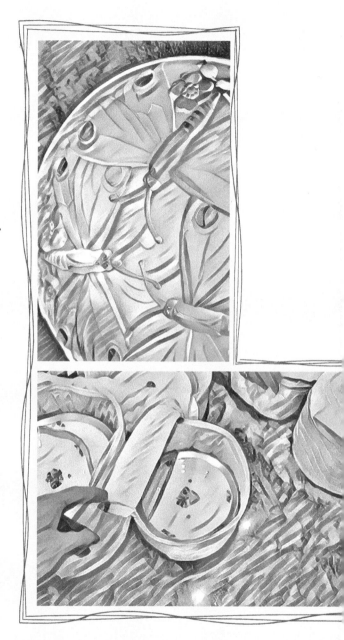

Stephie's great-grandmother was a Cincinnati socialite of the 1920s and 1930s, and her dinner party table was both vast and splendid. Her husband was the president of the Bank of Cincinnati and he had many important business associates. One of Mrs. Barrington's responsibilities was to set a fine table in the large mahogany-paneled dining room near Fountain Square, and to supervise many fine courses of rich food. On the nights when guests had opera tickets, a light supper was served at 6 p.m. on a set of china Mrs. Barrington called the "Haviland Supper Service." It was delightful and fresh, in a delicate porcelain with pink roses on white, and it included an army of matching covered serving bowls and platters. Since opera evenings were frequent, Mrs. Barrington had two informal supper services, one Haviland and one Copeland Spode.

Mrs. Barrington had three formal dinner services, all consisting of at least six pieces for each place setting, with settings for 18 or 24 diners. A set with salad plates, bread and butter plates, and dinner plates, plus a cup and saucer and a soup bowl, was considered the most informal. A more formal dinner service also included two appetizer plates (one for meat dishes and one for fish), perhaps an aspic plate, a bone dish (if fowl was served), and two sizes of dessert plates.

When a female friend came to afternoon tea, Mrs. Barrington used a tea service in fine porcelain by Royal Bavaria, which included a coffeepot, a chocolate pot, a teapot, a waste bowl, a water pitcher, a milk pitcher, and two sugar bowls (one for cubed and one for granulated), as well as a lemon dish and a tea strainer. This set included a demitasse service of tiny cups and saucers, a large porcelain handled cake plate, and three small pedestal cake raisers, along with eight ice cream dishes, 12 fruit dishes and a fruit bowl, and 12 dessert plates.

On the other side of town, a junior bank executive's wife would have only one small tea service, one supper service, and one formal dinner service, the bare minimum a service for 12 diners. Certain patterns were considered appropriate for one's income level and the time of day one dined.

Stephie's mother, Sarah, inherited five sets of china that had been delivered to her suburban Cincinnati home in 1987, packed in large wooden wine barrels stuffed with sawdust. Sarah had only liked one set, which Stephie remembered using on holidays. Stephie was never allowed to wash the dishes, and she had to use a special wooden knife if she wanted to cut anything on her plate.

Sarah was talking lately about sending all those services to Durham, as Stephie had been married for about three years and had settled in a downtown loft. Stephie listened to her mom's plans, and mentioned to her that "things have really changed about eating with friends these days."

Stephie explained that when she and Peter had friends over for an evening, they had usually already eaten and simply enjoyed a few drinks in Stephie and Peter's loft before hitting the town. Or they would go out for an earlier dinner and then have drinks. In the three years since Stephie and Peter had lived in the loft, she had not once offered a meal to anyone but her husband. Formal communal dining at Stephie's house was unheard of.

Peter had grown up in Mississippi and had been fascinated by his grandmother's glass-encased china closet, where the formal china lived. He was not allowed to open the doors, let alone touch the china. His grandmother was a stern great-granddaughter of a plantation owner.

Stephie and Peter discussed what it would mean to entertain with a formal china service. Stephie said, "I'd be afraid to use it." Peter said, "I'd break a piece and hate myself." Stephie said, "I'd rather give it all away than break anything." Peter pointed to the microwave and the dishwasher and cocked a mischievous eyebrow. Stephie replied to his unasked question, "No, of course we can't put any of it in those." Peter mentioned his boss was talking about transferring him to Silicon Valley in a few years. Stephie mentioned how difficult china is to pack and move. And then you have to insure it!

Sarah began to look into the value of each of the five elaborate services she had inherited from her grandmother, just in case Stephie didn't want all five. She learned that sets of fine china are one of the lowest valued things on the market. This a reflection of the buying power of Millennials, but also of Americans' modern attitudes about mealtimes. Dining rooms all over the country are becoming anything but dining rooms, repurposed into playrooms, offices, or even bedrooms. Those beautiful services are fast becoming a thing of the past, with little earning power on the secondhand market.

Stephie's mom called back, desperate to persuade the young couple: "How about Thanksgiving? Surely, you would have fun showing off a set when your brother and Sherry and the kids (all seven) come for Thanksgiving dinner. Stephie mentioned that it had been years since she or any of her friends had celebrated Thanksgiving with blood relatives. "Thanksgiving is for friends, Mom, since everyone goes home to their mom and dad's for Christmas. We call it 'Friendsgiving' these days."

Her mom was silent on the other end in Cincinnati. Stephie continued, "There's not just one residence for Friendsgiving, it's a roaming holiday. And it's almost always a potluck. If china dishes are actually brought out, they are stacked on the edge of the kitchen counter closest to the turkey. It's buffet-style, we eat off our laps."

With a certain quality of revenge, Peter thought of his hand being spanked away from his grandmother's creamer. His expression said it all. Stephie looked at Peter. Stephie said, "No thanks, Mom!"

Chapter 2

Elizabeth's Five Piles Theory of Divesting

You know you have to do it. I knew I had to. I was facing a storage locker that started nine years ago at $150 a month, rising to $200, then $250, $300, and finally $350 a month. That's when I knew I *had* to divest.

For someone who consults with clients on what's valuable, you'd think I'd know better, but I couldn't help myself: I collected stuff. Finally, I sat down in front of objects, furniture, clothing that had not seen the light of day in nine years, and I cried. So I made a plan. I closed and locked the storage locker and drove home. I thought, let's make space in the closets and garage and rooms of the house. Let's start with the house first! Maybe I'll find space in the house?

Wrong-headed thinking. If I really wanted what was in that storage locker, I would have fetched it home by now. I tackled "downsizing" the house first for all the wrong reasons, yet the result was both painstaking and great.

As I worked through the 10-month experience of divesting the house, and then the storage locker, I made notes on effective pile making. I practiced what I had told clients to do for years, and I created my Five Piles Theory. Think beyond physical piles of stuff; you'll find even a mental structure or typology helps you to downsize. You'll also want colored Post-It notes and your smart phone camera to keep records.

Pile 1
The High Rollers

This is your best pile. This is what will make you the most money when you decide to sell. Start by researching the objects in this pile. Consider the best things first, not last. Why? You'll learn about markets, auction houses, consignment terms, percentages, and how to research an object in a certain class. Once you have researching skills under your belt, the less valuable objects will be easy to research. Why spend hours researching an object worth $50? Think about what your time is worth, and pick "research-worthy" objects first.

Photo: Jan Reifenberg Collection

Pile 2
The Fine Donations

This is what you hope to donate to an organization that specializes in this class of objects: art to an art museum, vintage clothing to a theater, or pianos to schools. A hint: the IRS is less likely to examine your claim of a non-cash charitable contribution if they see the objects you are donating match the mission of the charity; for example, fine antique books to a library or vintage photos to a historical society. When you donate this pile, you'll need to call a certified appraiser to write your non-cash charitable contribution appraisal for your tax deduction.

Pile 3
The Family Jewels

This is what you intend to earmark for your heirs. Please refer to the opening chapter, "The Top Ten Objects Your Kids Do Not Want," where I describe how I (did not) consult with my son on what he and his wife wanted. Make a descriptive video tour, in which you talk about the prospective inherited objects, and send photos along with the video. Then set a time limit. Say, "Give me your decision in three months if you want the painting." After that, it's gone. If you have more than one grown child, send the video and photos to each one. Whoever gets back to you first gets what they want (within reason).

Once you have a list of what each kid wants, you can start an equitable distribution list based on worth and/or value. (Appraisers often get involved at this point.) And note those two words (worth and value) might mean something different to each grown child.

NO THANKS MOM

Pile 4
Your Keepers

Now is the perfect time to videotape or shoot photos of those objects you know you'll keep, because I bet you have not documented those for your homeowner's insurance! Make sure that the photos of your keepers include evidence that those objects are in your house. If you have a loss, insurance companies must be shown proof of ownership. There's nothing better than a photo of an object to do this; it's even better than a sales receipt. I suggest you spend one Saturday opening up every closet and drawer and taking a few pictures of their interiors. You don't need to take things out.

I also advise you take a video of yourself showing off your keepers and explaining their history and why you love them. Send that video to your grown children too. Someday they'll treasure your words on your favorite objects, even if they don't actually want them.

Now, send the videos of your keepers to your insurance agent with a letter stating that these are the appreciable objects in your house. Ask if it's time for a professional appraisal, or time to update your personal property line in your homeowner's insurance. This especially applies if you are downsizing for a move. Mover's insurance is deplorable. You will need this photo record if you are using a moving service, believe me, and you may need additional coverage from your homeowner's insurance company.

Pile 5
The Piddly Smalls

Instead of beginning with the garage sale objects, end your downsizing work with these objects of little value. Low-value objects take up the greatest psychic space. If you were to begin your downsizing project by making a pile of objects worth less than $50 and sticking them in your garage, every night you'd wake up at 4 a.m. and think, "In the morning I'm going to save Aunt Esther's ceramic chicken. I won't get anything for it anyway." And the chicken would reappear in your house. In no time, the whole pile in the garage would be back in the house. So end your project with the smalls. Leave the little stuff for the last week or weekend of your downsizing effort, and schedule a pick-up service to come the very next day to take it away to your eBay sales helper or the nearest charity thrift store.

Do not consider mounting a garage sale. You'll waste your time. Do you want to have the public beating down your doors at 5 a.m.? Do you want to spend three days of hard labor with unappreciative bargainers for $1,000? Pay someone to haul the garage sale stuff to Goodwill or a similar thrift store. Do it quick and don't look back. Remember—the smaller the object, the lesser the value, the larger the psychic space. Repeat that mantra!

Chapter 3

The Ten Valuable Habits of Successful Downsizers

The noted Zen philosopher Alan Watts said, "A universe of objects is objectionable." I think your grown children will agree. Throughout this guide, I have included case studies of real life divesting scenarios that illustrate Dr. Watts's sentiment. Whether you are moving to a smaller house or just lightening your load, remember your accumulations are YOUR accumulations. You may not really know or even understand your offspring's taste, but it is OK to let that be. What you have treasured for your kid's sake is not what your Millennial will remember about you. Yes, your objects have defined the quality of your life, but not its essence.

Attitudes about home have changed. When I remember my Oma's kitchen, I picture her china and distinctive aluminum pots and pans. However, your grown children may not have such a permanent vision of the family home. And for tangible reasons: we increasingly change living quarters and living partners. Your grown children have learned from us not to be nostalgic, or burdened by material memory-joggers. Moreover, the concept of *value* has changed; value is no longer gauged by worth. Value has a greater meaning today and is often gauged by ease of life, adaptability, status, style, utility, functionality, and short-term pleasure.

Here are 10 of the habits I've observed in the most successful downsizers. (When purging a collection, I like to think of the expression "Does it matter?" as a reflection on "matter"—the material things of life.)

1. Downsizers make a plan. It might sound like this: "Every weekend I will devote at least four hours straight to one of my tasks." (If you like my Five Piles Theory, this might result in one pile every three weekends.) The plan is not too big; it's just four hours a week. Go to your calendar after you have completed those four hours on a Saturday. Mark that Saturday with a big 4—you did it! You're getting the job done!

2. Downsizers make a visual picture, either mentally or in scrapbook form, of how the house should metamorphose. If you're moving, make a sketch of your new house and virtually place your furniture inside the house. If you are staying, sketch a picture of how you dream each room should look.

3. Downsizers appreciate that each house and each room within a house create a different tonal quality of light. So if you're moving, bring a piece of fabric you used in your old house to the vicinity or interior of your new house. Notice how the colors are different. Do the same with a small piece of furniture to see how the wood tones change. Personally, I did not follow my own suggestion the last time I moved. I moved from a small, solid, Spanish Colonial style adobe cabin up in the mountains to a 1962 open-plan vintage villa. I didn't check the light quality. All my furniture that I had earmarked to save looked appalling in the clear light and geometric windows of my new home. I had paid $3,000 to move that furniture to the new house, and I gave it all to Catholic Charities.

4. Once downsizers decide to donate something, they donate it. They don't rethink it. Period.

5. Once downsizers decide to sell something, either they find an expert who sells online or they (perhaps inadvisably) attempt to become an expert themselves. You will spend many hours becoming an expert. Downsizers take advantage of real experts, which includes hiring someone to take stuff to a flea market, eBay sellers, appraisers, auctioneers, estate sales companies, and book antiquarians. Effective downsizers don't try to learn all about each object class in a busy moving month.

6. Downsizers avoid involving spouses as much as possible. And if the spouse needs to downsize a specific collection, a gentle timeline is in order, as well as a prospective contract for a storage locker if the timeline fails. It has been my experience that between partners, there's one "stuff" person and one "non-stuff" person. Thus, two people completing their plans for their stuff by moving day is an unreachable dream. Look into a truck, a driver, and short-term storage.

7. If there's something you can't bear to part with, don't. I advise downsizers to have a MAYBE pile, which might need to go into storage to appease that little thought in your head: "Maybe I will still want these objects." The objects will prove themselves worthy (or more often than not, unworthy) in a few months. Just don't wait nine years like I did. Set a time limit.

8. Good downsizers take advantage of the IRS non-cash charitable contribution form, 8283, which lets you declare your own value of donated objects up to (what I advise) $2,000. The true ceiling (above which you are required to retain a certified appraiser) is $5,000 in fair market value (at time of printing). It has been my experience that taxpayers are least accurate assessing the value of objects in the $2,000 to $5,000 donation range, because that's the valuation point with the greatest margin for amateur research error.

9. Once an object is in the garage to be donated or sold, a downsizer will not visit that object after having a glass of wine.

10. A downsizer researches one charitable organization that will pick up with its own truck and will take almost everything when the task threatens to destroy health, relationships, pocketbooks, and peace of mind. Let that charity be your ace in the hole.

Conclusion

Your Kids and Grandkids are "Taste-Shifters"

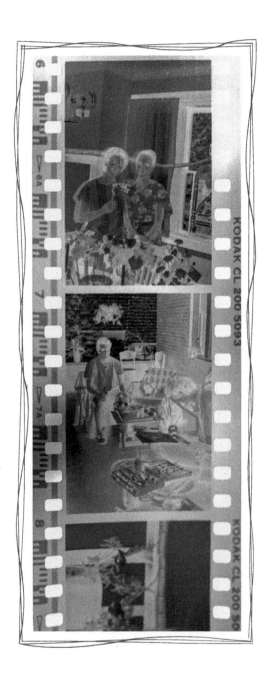

A generational and cultural shift happened across America when you and I were not looking. We Baby Boomers have discovered that our children and grandchildren have little desire to take in family treasures and lifetime collections that may have passed through generations. I have confronted this situation with many of my clients; certain possessions we saved have little appeal to the grown children for whom we did the saving. This might not amuse you if you are trying to convince your newly married son to take your favorite fine china service(s), formal crystal, linens, and silver (for which you have been racking up the storage locker fees).

I see that children and grandchildren do not have the space or the decorating aesthetic for antiques, collections, books, china, and family souvenirs, and many would sell their parent's objects if they received them, no matter their income level. It's a phenomenon that spans across state lines; the list of what today's kids don't want is the same all over the country. You and I may have been eager to receive our grandmothers' fine crystal; our kids dread the day.

This is because fine objects saved for the kids don't tend to work in their 21st-century homes. You have to face facts! Your grown children value a mobile lifestyle, uncluttered comfort, and the aesthetics of prevailing technology. Many grown children are proud collectors of certain categories of objects, but not the objects we valued at their ages. When I was collecting great artists, I never imagined that technology would become an asset class in the way of fine art.

I know many of my clients have good, if not great, art. But your grown children may have walls full of photos, and they don't want to remove their memories from their trek across Europe for your large landscape paintings of Europe. I collected fine English and French 18th-century furniture. Like mine, your grown children want furniture that is functional, not huge, dark, and difficult to maintain. I would bet that your grown children admire furnishings with clean lines; if you want to pass on any furniture from your house it better be mid-century modern. My grown son would rather have a comfortable modern sectional than a wood-trimmed antique settee. Who's to say our grown children are wrong?

If you want to give appreciated gifts of objects from your home, plan your downsizing in advance with a few of my hints, and get your offspring involved via the technology they use daily: photos, videos, and emails with bullet-pointed lists.

Present your objects to them in a language they can relate to: the language of images, not histories.

My mom left me objects in her will, and I didn't think I had a choice but to adopt them into my home. Today, "heirship" is different, perhaps because we are living longer, or because we just have more stuff. Our well-loved objects are now our problem, not our kids' problem. Thus, we must solve what to do with the objects our grown children will not appreciate inheriting and the solution does not involve sending them surprise packages! (No sneak attacks in the mail; don't you dare! I tried it, and it doesn't work!)

A Postscript

If you are a parent or grandparent and you disagree with me regarding my Top Ten Objects Your Kids Do NOT Want, I want to hear from you! That's because I predict trends will drastically change around material objects, especially those that are inheritable. This book was researched in 2017 from a large cross-section of my Boomer clients and their grown children, but as tastes and times change, these categories will change. And each category has exceptions, such as the son of a client of mine who eagerly awaits his mom's old electronic gear, or a client who tells me her four daughters all want her cedar chest. Another client's daughter runs a catering and formal china rental business, and would gladly buy up that orphaned formal china. (This is a reflection of the Millennial market that would rather rent than be encumbered.)

Because I have a doll phobia, I intentionally left dolls out of my Top Ten, but a doll collection is one of the hardest things to give to your grown children. I field many bewildered requests for help in evaluating dolls. Unless dolls are 1) in extremely good condition, 2) over 150 years old, 3) ethnic and with anthropological value, AND 4) including their original hair and clothing, they are rarely salable. Sadly, the 1980s and '90s saw "collectible" dolls marketed to TV shoppers and ladies' magazine readers. There's no market for these, and they often must be donated. My hint for evaluating dolls is to study the back of the necks for maker's marks, and then to email photos to an auction house, such as Dan Morphy's, which specializes in rare toys.

Objects occupy space that evokes places; they are symbols that bind the viewer to a specific location

and time. I purposefully use the word *bind* because the Millennial generation feels the tension in those ties that bind. That's why the word *heirloom* is so evocative, with the root *loom*; heirlooms are objects that are meant to weave your story around your heirs. Yet as the Millennial generation moves away from physical narratives of tangible objectification, they have become masters in picturing history in purely visual images. Therefore, the image of an object may often stand in for the object itself. Many of my Boomer clients tell me that their heirs want a photo archive of their parents' homes and the objects they contain.

This shift in the symbolic representation of the past is the crux of this book. Don't take personally the denial of your stuff, and remember, you aren't alone in this struggle: the denial is a reflection of a generational shift in picturing time, a shift that is a reflection of an inevitable generational adjustment in values. You might reflect upon this shift when you hear "No thanks, Mom."

THE PERSONALITY OF THE AMERICAN HOME —

Traditionalists, aka "The Silent Generation"

(born 1928-1945)

Baby Boomers

(born 1946-1964)

	Traditionalists, aka "The Silent Generation" (born 1928-1945)	Baby Boomers (born 1946-1964)
Who are they?	Babies of the Great Depression Space conquest youths Committed to spouse, country and corporation	American Dream babies Post-War, Cold War, and sexual revolution babies Highest divorce rate and second marriage rate in history
What are their priorities?	Goal oriented Pocketbook conscious Family and group centered	Children and youth centered Big spenders Self-improvement focused Status oriented
What do their houses say to you?	Be respectful and stable: home is our anchor.	Be either needed or important.

GENERATIONS OF PEOPLE WHO OWN "STUFF"

Gen Xers
(born 1965-1980)

Millennials*
(born 1981-1997)

Babies of working moms	Babies of divorce and the recession
Video game babies	Digital media natives
First generation to experience an economic downturn	The center of economic and environmental universe, for better or worse
Globally minded	Personally focused
Big spenders	Balanced spenders
Education and technology focused	Civic-ideal centered
Anti-status oriented	Socially oriented and socially critical
Be worthy, interesting, and valuable.	Be creative and bright. Act with integrity.

Traditionalists, aka "The Silent Generation"
(born 1928-1945)

Baby Boomers
(born 1946-1964)

	Traditionalists	Baby Boomers
Who's welcome?	Family and long-term friends (by invitation)	People who matter or who need help; their kids and their kids' friends
What is "home" to them?	Dependable space, maintained over time. Home is an institution.	Home is a status symbol
When is it "Home"?	"6 p.m. homes"	"8 p.m. homes"
Gifting style	Thoughtful gifters	Status gifters
Housekeeping style	Self-maintained spaces, with mom as housekeeper, dad as odd-jobber	Delayed housekeeping; housecleaning low on the list

NO THANKS MOM

Gen Xers

(born 1965-1980)

Millennials

(born 1981-1997)

Worthy people, guests with similar interests and education	Supportive people, fellow travelers, extended family, heroes
Self-curated, "skilled" home, "pricey" home	Home is a flexible, multitasking, social space.
"24/7 homes"	"5 p.m. homes"
Informational gifters	Whimsical gifters
Hired-out housekeeping	Flexible, shared housekeeping
Dumpers of clutter	Floors as "catch-all" spaces

THE PERSONALITY OF THE AMERICAN HOME

Traditionalists, aka "The Silent Generation"

(born 1928-1945)

Baby Boomers

(born 1946-1964)

Types of objects in the home

"Paid for" merchandise

Collectors of models, series, similar types of objects

Respect for the old and time-honored

Objects of obligations and tradition

Objects for routines and chores

"Honoring" objects, group identity, history, and sentimental objects

Lifetime owners of objects

"Family tree" objects

"Credit" merchandise

Collectors of "recognition" objects

"Look at me" and youth-related objects

Impressive objects, such as sports memorabilia and expensive wines

Lovers of non-routine objects

Unconventional or counter-culture collectors

Displays of the unique and special

Objects that stand for relationships

Brand name objects

Collectors of adventure-related objects

"Life's victory" collections

Gen Xers
(born 1965-1980)

Appreciable merchandise

Collectors of information and
educational objects

Favorite brand objects, such as
must-have technology

Anti-institutional collections

Educated connoisseurs, entitled to the best

Need-based objects

Kitchen gear

Non-sentimental gadgets

Leisure and open-space objects

Collections of grunge or DIY
objects, children's technology

Collections merged with
partner's collections

"Moneyed" objects and good clothing

Millennials
(born 1981-1997)

Smart merchandise, the "latest" objects

Collectors of experience-
related objects and images

"The Personal Touch" objects

Home and workspace objects mixed

Woodsy/natural objects

Game-related objects

Unique, sustainable baby
clothes and kid gear

Friend-centered purchases

"Responsible" socially aware objects

Networked objects

Fun, non-authoritative objects

Humble objects and creative,
handmade objects

Antique accents, grandparents' shrines

Traditionalists, aka "The Silent Generation"

(born 1928-1945)

Baby Boomers

(born 1946-1964)

Spaces

Traditionalists	Baby Boomers
Organized interior settings	Suspicious of parent's spaces and style
Nuclear family spaces	Child or team-centered spaces
Community spaces (pool, barbecue, tennis)	Spaces as status markers
Owned and paid for spaces	Two homes
Complete home/work separation	Shared spaces with partners
Quality, long-term spaces	Quality or conspicuous environments
Household work spaces and hobby spaces	Work and family spaces distinct
Hierarchical spaces	Youth spaces: kid's rooms, game room, entertainment centers
Institutionalized spaces: dining room, TV room	Communication spaces (phones on 24/7)
"Follow the rules" spaces	Spaces for framed photos, diplomas, awards, club and group affiliations
Dedicated spaces for certain objects, such as printed materials, garden and housekeeping materials, china	Curators of objects which show upward mobility
Spaces for both resourceful objects and retained objects	

Gen Xers
(born 1965-1980)

Millennials
(born 1981-1997)

Originated in mom's home, but moved
around; home is ambiguous

Calming spaces

Themed spaces for shared interests

Streamlined spaces

Independent, not interdependent spaces

Entrepreneurial spaces

Home as sanctuary

Self-sufficient productive spaces

Project and craft spaces

Casual, elegant spaces, with great kitchens

Fun spaces

Rooms as individualized technology spaces

Short-term homes, rentals

Leisure space, outdoor living space

Diverse communities

Cooperative homes, merged space

Techno-space: non-material, wired media

Multi-tasking space

Individual stamp on living
spaces: photos of "me/us"

Stimulating environments

Long-term relationship space

Fun, creative spaces, sheds,
studios, offices, kitchens

Easy spaces for shared fun,
food, music, media

Space for photos, natural objects,
pets, relationship markers

"Work from home" spaces

Traditionalists, aka "The Silent Generation"

(born 1928-1945)

Baby Boomers

(born 1946-1964)

Ideal home

Single family house in a stable community of similar people	After-work space in upper class community with personalized amenities and entertainment
A "good" address	Easy commute
Close to leisure activities	Quiet, unobtrusive neighbors

References:

Allen, Renee. (2007). Generational Differences Chart. Retrieved from http://www.wmfc.org/uploads/GenerationalDifferencesChart.pdf.

Bachman, J. G., Johnston, L. D., & O'Malley, P. M. (2014). *Monitoring the Future: Questionnaire responses from the nation's high school seniors, 2012.* Ann Arbor, MI: Institute for Social Research. Retrieved from http://www.monitoringthefuture.org/datavolumes/2012/2012dv.pdf.

Henderson, Steve. (2014, November 3). Spending Habits by Generation [Blog post]. Retrieved from https://blog.dol.gov/2016/11/03/spending-habits-by-generation.

*Pew Research Center. (2015, September 3). *Most Millennials Resist the 'Millennial' Label.* Retrieved from http://www.people-press.org/2015/09/03/most-millennials-resist-the-millennial-label/2/.

Gen Xers
(born 1965-1980)

Millennials
(born 1981-1997)

International style

Easy commute to good restaurants
and excellent daycares

Mid-century modern style, or
downtown Boho style

Alternative living spaces, rented spaces

Restored houses, farms, tiny houses

Cooperative work/live communities,
no garage necessary

Photo by Santi Visalli

About the Author

Elizabeth Stewart, Ph.D. is a 30-year "stuff" veteran, a certified member of the Appraisers Association of America. She analyzes art and antiques for estate planning to ascertain value, and is one of few appraisers nationally qualified in donation appraisals for charity for IRS deduction purposes. She advises on the best places to sell "stuff," and why certain things are worth keeping.

Her favorite career challenges have included the late Jonathan Winters estate of 160,000 objects, a dot-com executive's university donation of 20 truckloads of virtual reality, and a 50-year historical research archive of a Guggenheim fellow donated to UCSB. She can also tell you that your formal dinner china is worth NOTHING to your kids.

Elizabeth studies people whose stuff is attached to them. She holds a BA magna cum laude from Tufts University, a Master's in Historic Preservation from University of San Diego, and a Doctorate from Pacifica Institute in Mythological Studies with an Emphasis on Material Culture; her dissertation title, *The Material Image: Why Collectors Collect* is a scholarly approach to consumers, collectors, connoisseurs and hoarders. A journalist of 'stuff' as well, *"Ask the Appraiser"* appears weekly in the *Santa Barbara News Press* under the pseudonym "The Gold-digger"; she hosts a weekly radio show covering the arts on KZSB. Her first book, *The Savvy Appraiser: Collect Value Divest*, relates tales of the various categories of objects that people both collect and want to sell. Her second book, *NO THANKS MOM: The Top Ten Objects Your Kids Do Not Want (and what to do with them)* relates tales of the generational conflicts around inheritable objects.

Printed in the USA
CPSIA information can be obtained
at www.ICGtesting.com
LVHW071212011124
795362LV00021B/682

9 780998 102535